We Did It!

by Tristan Horrom
illustrated by Laura Logan

Decodable 18

McGraw Hill Education

Bothell, WA • Chicago, IL • Columbus, OH • New York, NY

MHEonline.com

Send all inquiries to:
McGraw-Hill Education
8787 Orion Place
Columbus, OH 43240

ISBN: 978-0-02-135404-7
MHID: 0-02-135404-9

Printed in China

10 11 12 13 14 DSS 28 27 26 25 24

Eve and Pete make a kite.

"It can be tan," he said.

"It can be big," she said.

Here is a rope.
Pete tapes it on.

She tugs on the kite.
Run, Eve, run!

The wind takes the kite up!
We did it!